| DATE DUE | | |
|---|---|---|
| | | |
| | | |
| | | |
| | | |
| | | |
| | | |
| | | |
| | | |
| | | |
| | | |
| | | |
| | | |
| | | |

**394.26**
**DEA**

**3 24571 0901565 5**
Dean, Sheri.

**Memorial Day**

*Our Country's Holidays*

# Memorial Day

## by Sheri Dean

Reading consultant: Susan Nations, M.Ed.,
author/literacy coach/
consultant in literacy development

**WEEKLY READER**®
PUBLISHING

**Please visit our web site at: www.garethstevens.com**
**For a free color catalog describing our list of high-quality books,**
**call 1-800-542-2595 (USA) or 1-800-387-3178 (Canada).**
**Our fax: (877) 542-2596**

Library of Congress Cataloging-in-Publication Data available upon request from publisher.
Fax (877) 542-2596 for the attention of the Publishing Records Department.

ISBN-10: 0-8368-6507-3   ISBN-13: 978-0-8368-6507-3 (lib. bdg.)
ISBN-10: 0-8368-6514-6   ISBN-13: 978-0-8368-6514-1 (softcover)

This edition first published in 2006 by
**Weekly Reader® Books**
An Imprint of Gareth Stevens Publishing
1 Reader's Digest Rd.
Pleasantville, NY 10570-7000  USA

Copyright © 2006 by Weekly Reader® Early Learning Library

Managing editor: Valerie J. Weber
Art direction: Tammy West
Cover design and page layout: Kami Strunsee
Picture research: Cisley Celmer

Picture credits: Cover, © A. Ramey/PhotoEdit; p. 5 © Skjold Photographs; p. 7
© Otis Imboden/National Geographic Image Collection; pp. 9, 11, 13, 15 © AP/Wide
World Photos; p. 17 © Tom Prettyman/PhotoEdit; p. 19 © David Young-Wolff/PhotoEdit;
p. 21 © Joe Raedle/Getty Images

Printed in the United States of America

3 4 5 6 7 8 9 10 09

## Note to Educators and Parents

Reading is such an exciting adventure for young children! They are beginning to integrate their oral language skills with written language. To encourage children along the path to early literacy, books must be colorful, engaging, and interesting; they should invite the young reader to explore both the print and the pictures.

In *Our Country's Holidays*, children learn how the holidays they celebrate in their families and communities are observed across our nation. Using lively photographs and simple prose, each title explores a different national holiday and explains why it is significant.

Each book is specially designed to support the young reader in the reading process. The familiar topics are appealing to young children and invite them to read — and reread — again and again. The full-color photographs and enhanced text further support the student during the reading process.

In addition to serving as wonderful picture books in schools, libraries, homes, and other places where children learn to love reading, these books are specifically intended to be read within an instructional guided reading group. This small group setting allows beginning readers to work with a fluent adult model as they make meaning from the text. After children develop fluency with the text and content, the book can be read independently. Children and adults alike will find these books supportive, engaging, and fun!

— Susan Nations, M.Ed., author, literacy coach,
and consultant in literacy development

On Memorial Day, we think about people who died for our country.

These people fought on land, on the seas, and in the air. They all wore different uniforms. They all tried to keep our country safe.

1959

Memorial Day is always on the last Monday in May. Many flowers bloom in May. We often use flowers to honor people who died for our country.

On Memorial Day, we put flowers on rivers, lakes, and seas. The flowers honor sailors who died at sea. We also put flowers and flags on graves.

11

We buy red paper flowers.
We wear the flowers to honor
our soldiers and sailors.

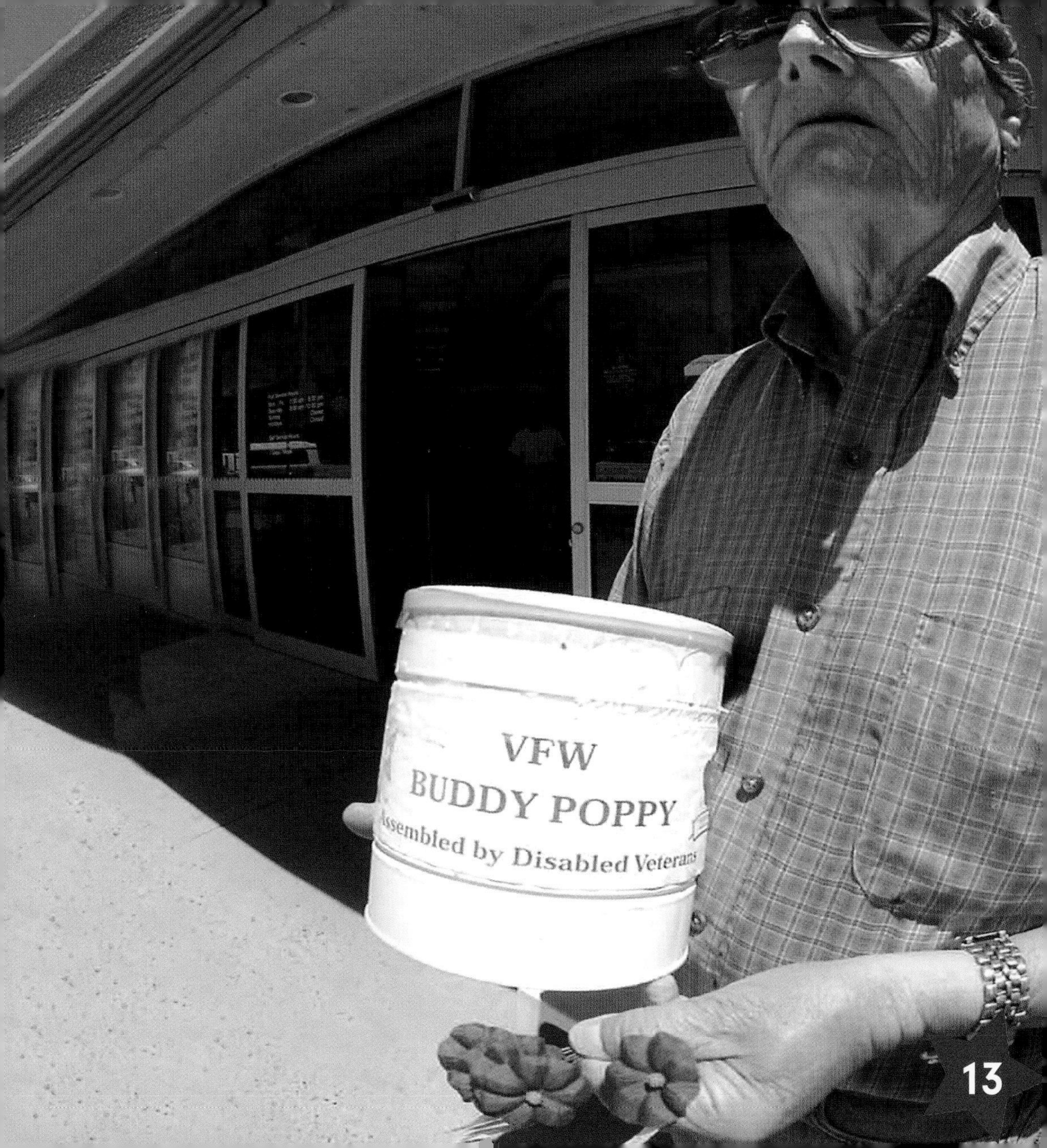
VFW
BUDDY POPPY
Assembled by Disabled Veterans

People fly flags halfway down the flagpole to honor people who have died. Putting the flag like this is called half-mast.

Many people watch parades. Soldiers, sailors, and other groups march in the parades.

17

On Memorial Day, we think about family and friends who died for our country.

On Memorial Day, we take a minute to be silent.  We often pray for world peace.

# Glossary

**flagpole** — a pole from which a flag flies

**graves** — places where people are buried

**half-mast** — a point about halfway down from the top of a flagpole

# For More Information

## Books

*Let's Get Ready for Memorial Day.* Lloyd Douglas (Sagebrush)

*Memorial Day.* Holiday Histories (series). Mir Tamim Ansary (Heinemann Library)

*Memorial Day.* Read about Holidays (series). Jacqueline S. Cotton (Children's Press)

*Memorial Day Surprise.* Theresa Martin Golding (Boyds Mills Press)

## Web Sites

Memorial Day
www.patriotism.org/memorial_day/
Learn about the history of the holiday and how we honor those who help our country.

23

# Index

## About the Author

**Sheri Dean** is a school librarian in Milwaukee, Wisconsin. She was an elementary school teacher for fourteen years. She enjoys introducing books and information to curious children and adults.